tomatoes

tomatoes

easy, delicious tomato recipes

Manisha Gambhir Harkins

Photography by Jean Cazals

RYLAND
PETERS
& SMALL

LONDON NEW YORK

First published in the USA in 2003
Ryland Peters & Small, Inc.
519 Broadway, 5th Floor
New York, NY 10012
www.rylandpeters.com

10 9 8 7 6 5 4 3 2 1

Text © Manisha Gambhir Harkins 2003
Design and photographs
© Ryland Peters & Small 2003

Library of Congress Cataloging-in-Publication Data
Harkins, Marisha Gambhir.
  Tomatoes : easy, delicious tomato recipes / Manisha Gambhir Harkins ;
photography by Jean Cazals.
    p. cm.
1. Cookery (Tomatoes) 2. Quick and easy cookery. I. Title.
TX803.T6 H37 2003
641.6'5642–dc21

                                        2002151581

Printed and bound in China.

Commissioning Editor Elsa Petersen-Schepelern
Editor Kathy Steer
Senior Designer Steve Painter
Production Deborah Wehner
Art Director Gabriella Le Grazie
Publishing Director Alison Starling

Food and Prop Stylist Louise Mackaness

Dedication To my sweet pea Billy and our wonderful clan—Susheela, Morag, Lakshman,
John, Lynne, Gordon, and little Daniel—for all of your love and affection.

Author's acknowledgments Hearty thanks to Sandra Purkess for testing a selection of
recipes at a moment's notice. Her innate skill and creativity deserve infinite praise.
Thanks also to my dear editor Elsa, for commissioning me for Round 2, and for always
remembering the salt and pepper when I don't! Thanks to Elizabeth for her patience
with my mad suggestions and for her great efforts all round; and finally Jean
Cazals and Louise Mackaness for gorgeous photography and styling.

Notes

All spoon measurements are level unless otherwise specified.

Uncooked or partially cooked eggs should not be served to the very young,
the very old or frail, or to pregnant women.

All meat, poultry, and eggs used in testing the recipes in this book were raised
free range, and all the vegetables were grown organically where possible,
which the author believes makes for better food and better health.

To sterilize preserving jars, wash the jars in hot, soapy water and rinse in boiling
water. Put into a large saucepan and cover with water. With the lid on, bring the
water to a boil and continue boiling for 15 minutes. Turn off the heat, then leave the jars
in the hot water until just before they are to be filled. Invert the jars onto clean kitchen
towels to dry. Sterilize the lids for 5 minutes by boiling. Jars should be filled and sealed
while still hot.

contents

simply the best ...

It's hard to imagine everyday cooking without tomatoes, whether raw, cooked, chopped and canned, or as a sauce. Even when they're not the main component of a dish, their unique signature is unmistakable.

Of course, everyone says that tomatoes don't taste the way they used to. They probably don't, because modern farming methods require varieties that can be picked, packed, transported, and sold without damage. That doesn't necessarily go hand-in-hand with flavor.

However, it is still possible to find tomatoes with that real old-fashioned flavor. Farmers' markets are the best source, and they're also sold at whole foods stores and some supermarkets. Look for the delicious heirloom varieties, or those based on the traditional Italian plum tomato. Small-fruited cherry or plum tomatoes seem to have more flavor, and even regular tomatoes have more taste if they're left to ripen on the vine.

But, however they're grown, tomatoes are still full of good things; plenty of vitamins A, C, and K, beta carotene, and lycopene. If you're a talented gardener (unlike me!), grow your own for optimum flavor and health.

baby tomato gazpacho

2½ lb. vine-ripened small tomatoes, such as cherry, Juliette, or Elfin

½ large red bell pepper, coarsely chopped

¾ teaspoon hot red pepper flakes or 1 fresh red chile, finely chopped, plus extra to serve (optional)

¼ teaspoon sweet smoked Spanish paprika (pimentón)

2 scallions, coarsely chopped

2 large garlic cloves, quartered

1 teaspoon sugar

⅔ cup extra virgin olive oil, plus extra to serve

2 tablespoons red wine vinegar

sea salt and freshly ground black pepper

to serve, your choice of:

1 green bell pepper, seeded and finely chopped

4 scallions, chopped

8 inches cucumber, peeled, seeded, and chopped

chopped fresh chives

chopped fresh basil

chopped fresh cilantro

serves 4

A traditional Spanish summer soup originally from Andalusia, gazpacho can be extremely good or terribly insipid, depending on the quality of the tomatoes and, to a certain extent, their consistency too. The secret is to use the sweetest, most intensely flavored tomatoes you can find (I prefer cherry or little Juliettes). I also use very little cold water—keeping the tomato flavor—plus lots of olive oil to make a richly sweet gazpacho. To serve, make your choice of toppings such as those listed, or chopped onion or chopped hard-cooked egg and small croutons.

Working in batches, put the tomatoes, pepper, chile, paprika, scallions, garlic, sugar, olive oil, vinegar, and ⅔ cup cold water in a blender and purée until completely smooth.

Press through a strainer into a bowl. Make sure you get all the liquid through and the skins are left behind. Add salt and pepper to taste and stir well. Chill for at least 1 hour, then ladle into bowls and sprinkle with finely chopped green bell pepper, scallions, cucumber, chile, if using, and herbs. Add a swirl of olive oil and serve.

Note I prefer my gazpacho cold but not chilled. Don't keep gazpacho too long—it should be served as fresh as possible.

appetizers, soups, and salads

insalata caprese
mozzarella, tomato, and basil salad

1 lb. fresh mozzarella cheese, preferably *mozzarella di bufala*, sliced or torn

8 vine-ripened plum tomatoes, such as Roma or San Marzano, thickly sliced

a large handful of basil leaves

best-quality extra virgin olive oil, for sprinkling

sea salt and freshly ground black pepper

Italian bread, such as ciabatta, to serve

serves 4

Insalata Caprese is a favorite Italian salad, sporting the colors of the national flag and just the simplest of dressings. Personally, I can think of nothing better than a little ground sea salt and pepper, and the traditional healthy sprinkling of the best sweet extra virgin olive oil. (Although color does not determine the quality of olive oil, green rather than golden oil looks great.)

Put about 3 slices or chunks of mozzarella on each plate. Add 3 slices of tomato, sprinkle with salt and pepper, then top with basil (basil should be torn, not cut, for best flavor and appearance).

Alternatively, arrange the tomato and mozzarella slices in lines on a large serving platter, then add salt, pepper, and basil leaves as before. Sprinkle olive oil generously over the salad and serve with plenty of Italian bread.

Variations

• Carefully sprinkle just a little balsamic vinegar over the salad.

• Pesto is a more robust topping, but don't use too much.

• Serve on a bed of peppery arugula leaves.

fattoush

3-4 white pita breads or other Middle Eastern flatbreads

1 romaine lettuce, leaves separated

3 medium, vine-ripened but still firm tomatoes, peeled

about 8 inches cucumber

4 scallions, thinly sliced diagonally

2 tablespoons finely chopped flat-leaf parsley

1 tablespoon finely chopped mint

dressing

1 large garlic clove, crushed

a large pinch of ground cinnamon

finely grated zest of 1 unwaxed lemon

1/4 cup cold-pressed extra virgin olive oil

2-3 tablespoons freshly squeezed lemon juice, or to taste

sea salt and freshly ground black pepper

serves 4

Fattoush is favorite Lebanese bread salad. Here is my version with a few extra ingredients added for extra color, texture, and flavor. You could leave the tomatoes unpeeled if you would like a more rustic effect.

Cut the pita breads in half, then toast them under a medium-hot broiler until they are starting to brown, but are still tearable, about 2 minutes on each side. Let cool briefly, then tear into bite-size pieces. Set aside.

Tear the lettuce into bite-size pieces and put in a large bowl. Cut the tomatoes into quarters, remove and discard the seeds, then cut each quarter into 4 slices. Slice the cucumber in half lengthwise. Using a teaspoon, scoop out the seeds and discard. Thinly slice the flesh, then add to the bowl. Add the tomatoes, scallions, parsley, and mint and mix well.

To make the dressing, put the garlic, cinnamon, lemon zest, olive oil, and lemon juice in a bowl and, using a small whisk, beat well. Season with salt and plenty of pepper. Pour the dressing over the salad and toss well. Just before serving, mix in the pieces of toasted pita bread.

spiced baked ricotta salata with tomatoes, pine nuts, and black olives

2 tablespoons finely chopped fresh herbs, such as basil or marjoram, plus 1 tablespoon extra to serve

a pinch of dried herbs, such as mint

¾ teaspoon zhatar, or a combination of toasted sesame seeds and dried thyme

1 lb. ricotta salata or farmer's cheese

freshly ground black pepper

topping

⅓ cup pine nuts, toasted

½ cup pitted black olives, chopped

8 oz. vine-ripened cherry tomatoes, halved

a few drops of Tabasco, to taste

extra virgin olive oil

sea salt and freshly ground black pepper

a shallow baking dish, lightly oiled

serves 4

Such an easy appetizer to delight your guests. It is very flexible—use your favorite fresh and dried herbs, or the ones I've used here. Experiment and enjoy. The topping is gloriously colorful against the speckled ricotta salata. Serve with a crisp salad and little grilled slices of Italian bread, grissini, toasted pita pieces, or crackers.

To make the topping, put the pine nuts, olives, cherry tomatoes, Tabasco, and herbs in a bowl and add salt and pepper to taste. Mix well, then sprinkle with enough olive oil to coat. Mix again and set aside.

Preheat the oven to 400°F. Put the herbs, spices, and pepper in a bowl and stir well. Put the whole cheese in the prepared dish and gently press the mixture all over the top and sides of the cheese. Bake for 18–20 minutes or until lightly browned on top, and sizzling but still firm.

Either leave the cheese in the dish or transfer to a warmed serving dish. Add the topping and serve.

Variations

• Add spinach and extra baked cheese to make an entrée for lunch.

• Use the topping as a dressing for cheese and salad.

italian bean and tomato soup with parsley and sage oil

1 tablespoon butter

1 tablespoon extra virgin olive oil

2 bay leaves

3 slices bacon, trimmed of excess fat, then finely chopped

1 medium leek, thinly sliced

1 carrot, finely chopped

2 lb. canned pinto beans, rinsed and drained, about 4 cups

1/2 cup chopped canned tomatoes

1 teaspoon tomato paste

4 1/2 cups chicken stock

2 sprigs of flat-leaf parsley and 1 sprig of sage, tied together with kitchen twine

freshly ground black pepper

2 cups vine-ripened small-fruited plum tomatoes, such as Juliette, halved, to serve

parsley and sage oil

a small bunch of flat-leaf parsley, tough stalks discarded

a few sage leaves

1/2 cup extra virgin olive oil

serves 4

This soup has a decidedly Italian flavor and is one of my favorites—easy, versatile, and nourishing. Sage is a strong herb, so use with care. It adds its lovely aroma to the soup, but if you prefer, you could make the oil just with parsley.

To make the parsley and sage oil, put the parsley, sage, and olive oil in a blender and pulse until well mixed—don't worry if it is slightly textured. Set aside until ready to use.

Heat the butter and olive oil in a medium saucepan. Add the bay leaves and bacon and sauté briefly. Add the leeks and carrots and cook gently until the leeks soften. Add the beans, tomatoes, tomato paste, chicken stock, parsley, and sage sprigs. Bring to a boil, lower the heat, and simmer gently for 10 minutes. Cover and cook for a further 10–15 minutes or until the carrots are tender.

Reserving the bacon, put a few ladles of the beans and vegetables in a blender and purée until smooth. Pour back into the saucepan, season to taste with pepper, stir well, and reheat.

Ladle the soup into 4 warmed bowls, top with the halved plum tomatoes, sprinkle with the parsley and sage oil, and serve.

Note If you have access to an Italian gourmet shop that imports direct from Italy, ask them for borlotti beans. They are even more delicious, and would be traditional for this soup.

tomato and anchovy bruschetta

8 oz. small-fruited tomatoes,
such as Juliette, about 2 cups,
quartered

8 anchovies, chopped

¼ teaspoon dried oregano

2 tablespoons finely chopped
flat-leaf parsley

4 thick slices day-old crusty, close-
textured bread, such as ciabatta

2 large garlic cloves, halved

best-quality extra virgin olive oil

freshly ground black pepper

serves 4

Simple dishes are often the most delicious—sweet tomatoes, herbs, and the best olive oil you can find, what more can you want?

Put the tomatoes, anchovies, oregano, and half the parsley in a bowl and mix well. Season generously with pepper.

Heat a stovetop grill pan over high heat, add the slices of bread, and cook for 40–60 seconds on each side until golden brown and barred with grill marks. Rub both sides of the bruschetta with the garlic.

Put the bruschetta on 4 plates and spoon the tomato and anchovy mixture over the top. Sprinkle with a little olive oil and the remaining parsley and serve at once.

Note I don't advocate peeling small-fruited tomatoes as a rule, but it's not too much trouble if you are very particular. With any little tomatoes, cut a cross in the skin, drop them in a bowl of boiling water, and let soak for 8–10 seconds. Remove the tomatoes from the bowl with a slotted spoon, let cool slightly, then remove the skins. They just slip off.

grilled goat cheese salad
with tomato balsamic dressing

8 oz. mixed salad greens

14 oz. chèvre blanc or other goat cheese with rind, cut into 4 rounds

2 avocados

3/4 cup pecan halves, toasted

sea salt and freshly ground black pepper

tomato balsamic dressing

1 tablespoon sugar

1 teaspoon tomato paste

2 tablespoons balsamic vinegar

6 tablespoons extra virgin olive oil

2 vine-ripened medium tomatoes, seeded and finely chopped

serves 4

Goat cheese, broiled until oozingly good, was popularized by Alice Waters at Chez Panisse in Berkeley. Thanks to this restaurant, melting goat cheese salads appear in various guises around the globe. I like goat cheese with toasted pecans. The sharp tomato balsamic dressing cuts through the richness of the cheese and avocado, and the juice and seeds of the tomatoes add to the flavor of the dressing. I don't bother peeling the tomatoes, but it's entirely up to you.

To make the dressing, put the sugar and 1 tablespoon water in a small bowl. Whisk to dissolve the sugar, then beat in the tomato paste and balsamic vinegar, beating rapidly until thoroughly incorporated. Add the olive oil slowly, beating constantly, until emulsified. Add the tomatoes and mix well. Set aside.

Put the salad greens on 4 plates and add salt and pepper to taste. Heat a large nonstick skillet over medium-high heat, add the goat cheese slices, and cook until they start to bubble and brown in places, about 5 minutes.

Meanwhile, slice the avocados in half, remove the seeds, peel and thinly slice lengthwise, then arrange the slices over the salad greens. Sprinkle with the pecans and dressing. When the cheese is cooked, carefully lift a slice onto the center of each plate. Top with a little more dressing or serve separately. Serve at once.

pan-fried steak
with roasted tomato and rosemary sauce

4 small steaks, about 10 oz. each

1 tablespoon extra virgin olive oil

1 tablespoon unsalted butter

sea salt and freshly
ground black pepper

crisp green salad, to serve
(optional)

**roasted tomato and
rosemary sauce**

1 lb. vine-ripened cluster tomatoes,
on the vine

8 - 10 garlic cloves, unpeeled

3 - 4 sprigs of rosemary

1/3 cup extra virgin olive oil

yogurt mashed potatoes

2 lb. white or Yukon gold
potatoes, boiled

1 cup whole-milk plain yogurt

1 tablespoon butter

sea salt and freshly
ground black pepper

serves 4

Use either boneless sirloin or New York strip steaks and cook to your liking following the general rule of 2½ - 3 minutes each side for rare, 4 minutes each side for medium, and 5 - 6 minutes each side for well done, depending on thickness. The garlicky roasted tomato and rosemary sauce is perfect with most meats. It is also easy to make—you don't even have to peel the tomatoes.

To make the sauce, preheat the oven to 400°F. Spread the tomatoes, garlic, and rosemary in a roasting pan and sprinkle with olive oil. Cook for 20 - 25 minutes until slightly collapsed but not charring. Let cool slightly, then remove and discard all the stems and stalks. Put the tomatoes, garlic, rosemary, and roasting oil in a blender and purée until smooth. Press through a strainer into a small saucepan, then set aside and keep the mixture warm on top of the stove or in a low oven.

To make the yogurt mashed potatoes, put the cooked potatoes in a large bowl, add a spoonful of yogurt, and mash well. Continue adding the yogurt at intervals until all has been used and the mixture is smooth. Add the butter, salt, and pepper to taste, and mash again. Keep the potatoes warm.

Season the steaks with pepper. Heat a large, heavy skillet until hot. Add the oil and butter and, when bubbling, add the steaks and pan-fry to your liking, turning just once. Season with salt just before turning.

Serve the steaks with the yogurt potatoes, the tomato and rosemary sauce, and a crisp green salad, if using.

Note If you prefer to cook the steaks without any extra butter, use a nonstick pan or stovetop grill pan. Keep the heat high to sear the outside but produce a tender interior.

fish, meat and poultry

easy chicken tacos
with tomato and jalapeño salsa

3/4 teaspoon ground cumin

3/4 teaspoon pasilla chile flakes, or ground chiles, to taste

1/2 teaspoon paprika

1/2 teaspoon salt

1 lb. skinless chicken, finely chopped

1 tablespoon extra virgin olive oil

2 garlic cloves, crushed

8 taco shells

guacamole

2 large avocados, halved

1 garlic clove, minced

freshly squeezed juice of 1/2–1 lime

sea salt and freshly ground black pepper

to serve

shredded romaine lettuce

chopped scallions

1 recipe Tomato and Jalapeño Salsa (page 56)

sour cream or plain whole-milk yogurt (optional)

grated mature cheese, such as aged Monterey jack (optional)

serves 4

What really makes a taco, or other tortilla-based dish, is a great freshly made salsa. Different salsas have been invented over the past few decades, but here I use the classic red tomato salsa with which we are all familiar.

To make the guacamole, put the avocado flesh in a bowl and mash well with a fork. Add the garlic and lime juice and mix well. If making in advance, rub the cut lime over the top of the guacamole and brush with a little lime juice. Cover tightly with plastic wrap until ready to use.

Put the spices and salt in a bowl and mix well. Add the chicken and toss until well coated. Heat the olive oil in a wide, nonstick skillet, add the garlic, and sauté for 30 seconds. Increase the heat, add the chicken, and stir-fry for about 5 minutes or until the chicken is tender and cooked through with no traces of pink.

To serve, warm the taco shells in a hot oven. Divide the chicken between the taco shells and serve at once, letting guests fill their own shells with shredded lettuce, scallions, salsa, and guacamole. Top with a little sour cream or yogurt and grated cheese, if using.

Note Although the chicken is usually pan-fried on its own or with garlic, the flavor is more interesting if you rub it with hot red pepper flakes, paprika, and cumin. You can also rub whole chicken breasts with the spices and salt, then grill them and tear into strips before using in the tacos.

roasted monkfish tails provençale

2 large monkfish tails, about 1 lb. each

4-5 large garlic cloves, sliced into slivers

1 large onion, chopped

sprigs of herbs, such as winter savory, thyme, rosemary, chervil, or tarragon

1 1/2 tablespoons capers, rinsed and drained

1/2 cup pitted green olives, sliced (optional)

5 vine-ripened tomatoes, peeled, seeded, and chopped

2/3 cup white wine

extra virgin olive oil, for sprinkling

sea salt and freshly ground black pepper

serves 4

The monkfish tails are prepared in the way the French roast a leg of lamb—a fabulous idea with many possibilities. Here, the fish is studded in typical fashion with garlic slivers, then cooked in a melange of herbs, capers, tomatoes, and olives, making a truly fantastic dish.

Preheat the oven to 375°F.

Using a small sharp knife, pierce little holes in the monkfish tails and push in the garlic slivers. Pile the chopped onion in the middle of a roasting pan, then spread the herbs on top. Put the monkfish tails on top of that and season well with salt and pepper. Spread the capers, olives, if using, and tomatoes over the fish. Add the wine and sprinkle generously with olive oil.

Bake for about 25 minutes, basting at least once with the pan juices. Remove from the oven, slice into portions, and serve hot with your choice of vegetable accompaniments.

seared duck salad
with double tomato relish

4 heads Belgian endive, trimmed at
the base and leaves separated

4 large duck breasts, with skin

sea salt and freshly
ground black pepper

double tomato relish

3 tablespoons sun-dried tomato oil
(taken from the oil-packed jar of
sun-dried tomatoes below)

12 large shallots, sliced

14 sun-dried tomatoes packed in
oil, drained and chopped

1 lb. cherry tomatoes, quartered

1/4 cup apricot jam

a pinch of sugar, to taste (optional)

serves 4

A simple way to serve duck, with a sweet-tart relish that works well
with this meaty bird. This dual tomato condiment is a cross between
a relish and chutney, but far quicker to make than the latter. You
can also use the whole endive as a vegetable, braised with some
of the relish and an extra splash of olive oil. The leaves become
wonderfully mellow when treated this way, and the relish turns into
a warm sauce.

To make the relish, heat the sun-dried tomato oil gently in a small saucepan.
Add the shallots and cook gently for about 10 minutes. Add the sun-dried
tomatoes and cherry tomatoes and cook until they have just begun to soften
and the mixture starts to bubble and thicken.* Add the apricot jam and the
sugar, if using. Cook for 1 minute more, then let cool before using.

Using a sharp knife, make diagonal slashes into the skin of the duck breasts
without cutting through the flesh, then season with salt and pepper. Heat a
heavy skillet over medium-high heat, add the duck breasts, skin side down,
and cook for 5 minutes until the skin is crisp and golden. Turn the breasts
over and cook for 4 minutes more, or as rare as you like. (You may have to
cook the duck in batches—don't overcrowd the pan.) Remove from the pan
and let rest for about 5 minutes in a warm place to set the juices.

Put the endive on 4 salad plates. Cut the duck crosswise into thick slices,
arrange on top of the endive, and top with 1 – 2 spoonfuls of relish. Serve.

*Note You can add the cherry tomatoes later so they hold their shape more.

spicy grill-pan scallops
with sweet roasted tomatoes and peppers

3/4 – 1 teaspoon ground coriander

12 large sea scallops
or 16 medium

1 large chile, seeded
and finely chopped

sea salt and freshly
ground black pepper

roasted tomatoes and peppers

1 lb. vine-ripened tomatoes
or ripe Brandywines

2 red bell peppers

1 yellow bell pepper

2 – 3 tablespoons
extra virgin olive oil

a pinch of ground ginger

a pinch of ground coriander

3/4 teaspoon sugar

to serve

4 generous handfuls of
mixed baby greens

crusty bread

serves 4

If it's the height of summer, look for heirloom tomatoes at farmers' markets. Brandywines are magnificent. Otherwise choose fragrant vine-ripened tomatoes. The sugar enhances the natural sweetness of the vegetables and is a good contrast to chile heat.

Put the coriander on a large plate, season with salt and pepper, and mix well. Rub the mixture over the scallops, then add half the chopped chile to the plate and roll the scallops in the chile until coated. Set aside for 30 minutes. Preheat the oven to 400°F.

Put the tomatoes and bell peppers in a roasting pan. Put the oil in a bowl, add the spices and remaining chopped chile, and beat well. Pour over the vegetables, then sprinkle the tomatoes with the sugar. Roast for 25 minutes, or until soft and just browned in places.

Meanwhile, heat a large, stovetop grill pan over high heat. Add the scallops and chiles and sear for 1 – 2 minutes, turning once, until the scallops are just cooked and barred with grill marks on both sides. Do not overcook or they will be tough.

Transfer the scallops and chiles to 4 heated plates, then add the roasted vegetables and a handful of salad greens. Sprinkle with some of the roasting juices and serve immediately with crusty bread.

rustic chicken panini with sicilian pesto

2 large ciabatta loaves

4 skinless chicken breasts

olive oil, for brushing

mixed salad greens

sea salt and freshly ground
black pepper

sicilian pesto

$1/2$ cup basil leaves

$1/3$ cup whole blanched almonds

$1/2$ cup freshly grated
Parmesan cheese

1 garlic clove, crushed

3 vine-ripened plum tomatoes, such
as Roma or San Marzano, peeled,
halved, and seeded

$1/2$ cup best-quality
extra virgin olive oil

sea salt and freshly ground
black pepper

serves 4

All types of pesto are available these days, and even though purists avoid all but the traditional green Ligurian-style, many alternatives also taste delicious. This one is from Sicily—the almonds are typical of the region and replace the pine nuts used in the north. Combined with gorgeous sun-ripened tomatoes, they make a pale red pesto, rustic and delicious.

To make the pesto, put the basil, almonds, Parmesan, and garlic in a food processor and blend until the almonds are coarsely chopped. Add the tomatoes then, with the motor still running, slowly pour in the olive oil. Pulse into a slightly textured, thick paste. Season to taste with salt and pepper and mix well.

Split the ciabatta loaves through their thickness, the cut in half, so each loaf is in 4 pieces. Toast the ciabatta, in batches, under a broiler until golden brown on both sides. Keep them warm.

Cut each chicken breast in half, then put between 2 sheets of plastic wrap. Using a rolling pin, beat evenly until each piece is about $1/2$ inch thick. Brush with olive oil and season with salt and pepper. Heat a stovetop grill pan until very hot. Add the chicken, reduce the heat and cook for 3 – 4 minutes on each side or until completely cooked through. Keep them warm.

To serve, spread a spoonful of pesto on the ciabatta, add a handful of salad greens, 2 chicken pieces, another spoonful of pesto, and another piece of ciabatta. Repeat to make the 3 other sandwiches, then serve.

Variation Various red pestos appear on the shelves—a popular one uses sun-dried tomatoes and the usual pine nuts, basil, garlic, and olive oil. Still others combine red peppers with tomatoes. Try them in this recipe.

hot thai shrimp and green tomato curry

1 tablespoon safflower or peanut oil

1/4 cup Thai green curry paste (preferably a Thai brand)

3-4 slices of fresh galangal or ginger

2 kaffir lime leaves, thinly sliced

1 stalk of lemongrass, outer leaves discarded, remainder very finely chopped

1 cup coconut milk

1 lb. uncooked shrimp, peeled, deveined, and shells reserved for the stock

7 green tomatoes, peeled and chopped into small chunks

palm sugar or brown sugar, to taste

4 scallions, thinly sliced

a handful of cilantro, chopped

a few Thai basil leaves (optional)

cooked fragrant Thai rice, to serve

quick hot stock

2 kaffir lime leaves

1 small hot chile, such as bird chile, halved lengthwise

1/4 teaspoon green peppercorns (optional)

1 stalk of lemongrass, bruised and split in half lengthwise

1 garlic clove

a few shallots, halved

serves 4

I have to admit I'm not a fan of fried green tomatoes, because there are many much more satisfying ways of using these unripe tomatoes. In Asia, from Thailand to India, green tomatoes are relished for their sourness and used in pickles, chutneys, and in dishes like this one, to add their unique tang. The juice and seeds are wonderfully tart—don't get rid of them! This is a seriously hot curry, so to reduce the heat, omit the green peppercorns and chile in the stock. Alternatively, reduce the amount of curry paste used or buy a milder one. My family, however, likes it just as it is!

To make the quick hot stock, put the reserved shrimp shells, lime leaves, chile, peppercorns, if using, lemongrass, garlic, and shallots in a saucepan with 1 quart water and bring to a boil. Lower the heat and simmer for about 30 minutes. Pour through a fine strainer into a bowl, reserving 1 1/2 cups for this recipe. Freeze any leftover stock for future use.

Heat the oil in a saucepan and add the curry paste. Stir-fry for several minutes, being careful not to burn. Add the reserved shrimp stock, galangal or ginger, lime leaves, and lemongrass. Bring to a boil, lower the heat, cover, and simmer gently for 2-3 minutes. Uncover and bring to a rapid simmer, add the coconut milk, stirring to keep it from separating. Lower the heat again and simmer gently for 10-15 minutes. Add the shrimp and cook for 2-3 minutes until just cooked (no longer or they will be tough). Add the tomatoes and cover for 1 minute until heated through. Add sugar to taste, then sprinkle with scallions, coriander, chives, and basil, if using. Serve with plenty of rice to soak up the heat.

Note If you don't have time to make shrimp-shell stock, use 1 bottle clam juice to 3 cups water. Add the remaining ingredients for the quick hot stock.

provençal beef and tomato daube

1 tablespoon unsalted butter

1 tablespoon extra virgin olive oil

1 large onion, coarsely chopped

3 garlic cloves, thickly sliced

2 lb. beef chuck, cut into cubes

8 oz. canned tomatoes

1 cup red wine

2 bay leaves

a few sprigs each of thyme and parsley tied together with kitchen twine (or other herbs to taste)

4 carrots, halved

about 1 3/4 cups beef stock

1/2 cup pitted olives, green, black, or both

4 oz. artichoke hearts in oil, drained

5-6 small, vine-ripened tomatoes, peeled, quartered, and seeded

sea salt and freshly ground black pepper

extra thyme and parsley, chopped, to serve (optional)

beurre manié

1 tablespoon unsalted butter

3 tablespoons cornstarch or flour

serves 4

A daube is a wonderful, slow-cooked Provençal beef stew traditionally cooked in a deep, covered, earthenware casserole called a daubière. The red wine and tomato combination results in a deliciously full-bodied sauce. If possible, try to make this dish in the morning, or even the night before, to develop the flavors. I make mine with organic ingredients, which I think give even more flavor. I serve the daube with boiled, buttered potatoes and sautéed Savoy cabbage. Comfort food!

Preheat the oven to 325°F.

Put the butter and oil in a large heavy skillet and heat until foaming. Add the onions and sauté gently until softened and translucent. Add the garlic and sauté briefly. Working in batches, add the beef to the pan and brown on all sides to seal—keep the pieces well apart so they sauté, not boil. Remove them to a plate while you brown the remaining pieces. Put all the pieces back in the pan, add the canned tomatoes and wine, and bring to a boil. Reduce the heat and simmer for 1 minute.

Meanwhile, put the bay leaves, herbs, and carrots in a deep pot or Dutch oven, then add the contents of the skillet. Add the beef stock, mix, and cover with a lid. Bring to a boil, season with salt and pepper, then immediately transfer the pot to the oven. Cook for about 3 1/2-4 hours until the beef is falling apart, stirring once or twice during the cooking time.

To make the beurre manié, mash the butter and cornstarch or flour together into a paste and form into several small balls.

Remove the pot from the oven. Strain the liquid into a saucepan, taste, and adjust the seasoning if necessary. Leave the meat and vegetables in the casserole. Beat the beurre manié into the liquid, one ball at a time, until the sauce is smooth and shiny. Heat through, beating well. Pour back into the pot. Just before serving, add the olives, artichokes, and tomatoes. Heat through and serve, sprinkled with the thyme and parsley, if using.

spicy tomato and harissa squid with vermicelli and parsley

1 1/2 lb. cleaned baby squid

8 oz. (3 bundles) rice vermicelli noodles

3 tablespoons extra virgin olive oil

5-6 tablespoons harissa paste, preferably rose harissa, or to taste

10 oz. small, vine-ripened tomatoes, quartered

a handful of flat-leaf parsley, finely chopped

sea salt and freshly ground black pepper

freshly squeezed juice of 1/2 lemon, to serve (optional)

serves 4

An unusual combination of ingredients, but resulting in a boldly satisfying dish lifted by North African flavors. The secret is to use a good harissa paste—spicy but with a hint of some delicate Moroccan flavors, such as in the rose harissa used here. If your harissa is mild to medium, then you may need to use several tablespoons. Adjust according to your heat preference. Small vine-ripened tomatoes are larger than cherries but smaller than regular vine tomatoes—they are available from most large supermarkets.

Pick over the squid and remove any hard pieces. Slice the bodies into thin rings and cut the tentacle bundles in half lengthwise. Set aside.

Put the noodles in a bowl, cover with boiling water, and let soak for 3-4 minutes or according to the package instructions.

Meanwhile, heat 2 tablespoons of olive oil in a wide skillet or wok. Add the squid and most of the harissa paste and sauté briskly, stirring well. Cook for just 1-2 minutes until the squid just loses its translucence – turning bright white and only just bouncy. Do not overcook or the squid will be tough.

As soon as the noodles are ready, drain them, quickly refresh in cold water, then transfer to a bowl. Add the remaining 1 tablespoon of olive oil and remaining harissa and mix with a fork until the noodles are coated. Add to the pan with the tomatoes, parsley, salt, and pepper. Toss well until heated through. Serve hot with a squeeze of lemon juice, if using.

Note   Wheat vermicelli noodles may also be used.

pizza margharita

This is probably the world's most famous pizza, supposedly created for Margharita, Queen of Naples, by the owner of a local pizzeria. Try these individual pizzas with a thin crust—simple yet sophisticated and extremely good.

3 cups all-purpose flour, plus extra for dusting

1 teaspoon salt

1/2 teaspoon sugar

2 teaspoons active dry yeast

3 tablespoons extra virgin olive oil, plus extra for oiling

topping

16 oz. canned whole plum tomatoes, chopped and drained well, about 2 cups*

16 basil leaves, green or purple

a pinch of sugar

8 oz. fresh mozzarella cheese, drained and cut into 12 slices

extra virgin olive oil, for sprinkling

sea salt and freshly ground black pepper

a large baking sheet, lightly oiled or dusted with cornmeal

serves 4

*Don't use canned chopped tomatoes—they have more juice and can make the pizza soggy.

Sift the flour, salt, and sugar into a large bowl and stir in the yeast. Add the olive oil and about 1 cup plus 1 tablespoon of warm water. Using a knife, mix well until the mixture forms a soft dough, adding a little extra water if necessary. Transfer the dough to a lightly floured work surface and knead for 5–10 minutes until smooth and elastic.

Lightly oil a large bowl with olive oil, put the dough in the bowl, and roll it around until well coated. Cover with plastic wrap and let stand in a warm place for 1–1 1/2 hours until doubled in size. Preheat the oven to 450°F.

Transfer the dough to a lightly floured work surface, punch down, and knead lightly for 1 minute, then divide into 4 balls. Take one ball and, using your hands or rolling pin, pat or roll out to 9 inches diameter. Transfer to the baking sheet. Repeat with the remaining dough to make 4 individual pizzas.

Spread the tomatoes over the dough, and put half the basil on top. Season with the sugar, salt, and pepper, then top each pizza with 3 slices of mozzarella. Let rise for a further 10–15 minutes until the crust puffs up, then sprinkle with olive oil. Bake in the oven for 8–10 minutes until the crust is crisp and golden. Sprinkle with the remaining basil and a little more olive oil. Serve at once.

Note To make the pizza dough in a food processor, sift the flour, salt, and sugar into the processor, then add the yeast. With the motor running, pour in the olive oil and about 1 cup warm water. Continue mixing, still on a slow speed, for 1–2 minutes until smooth and elastic. If the dough is too sticky or too dry, add a little more water or flour as necessary.

vegetarian entrées

provençal tomato tian

3 large zucchini, trimmed

a small bunch of fresh herbs
(or fresh herbes de Provence),
chopped*

1 small red bell pepper, halved,
seeded and sliced crosswise

1 lb. vine-ripened plum or other
flavorful tomatoes, cut into
wedges and seeded

1/3 cup extra virgin olive oil

2 garlic cloves, minced

sea salt and freshly ground
black pepper

crusty bread, to serve

a large ceramic tian or baking
dish, well greased with olive oil

serves 4–6

*Herbes de Provence usually
include oregano, thyme,
rosemary, savory, and marjoram,
which are the native summer
herbs of the region.

A tian is a Provençal baked dish named after the shallow ceramic dish in which it is cooked. You can use any combination of suitable vegetables, but the tomato is probably the one most associated with sunny southern France. Garlic and olive oil also mark this dish as unmistakably Mediterranean. This version is one of the simplest of tians— perfect for a fine summer's day.

Preheat the oven to 400°F.

Slice the zucchini diagonally into ovals, then arrange in the prepared dish in an overlapping layer. Sprinkle with some of the herbs. Add a layer of peppers, then a layer of tomato wedges. Sprinkle with the remaining herbs, salt, and pepper.

Put the oil and garlic in a bowl, mix well, then pour all over the vegetables. Bake for about 45 minutes or until tender.

Serve hot with crusty bread to mop up the garlicky oil.

baked eggplant and tomato stacks

extra virgin olive oil

1 eggplant, about 8 oz., sliced into 12 thick rounds

1 large beefsteak tomato, about 6 oz., sliced into 8 rounds

8 oz. Taleggio cheese, or any other good melting cheese, cut into 12 slices

crisp green salad or lightly steamed vegetables, to serve

a ceramic baking dish, oiled

serves 4

This is a filling vegetarian dish, topped with bubbly, browned cheese. I've used Taleggio cheese, which is full of nuttiness when melted, but use any other good melting cheeses, such as Fontina, Gruyère, or mozzarella. Beefsteak tomatoes are perfect for this dish as they are delightfully large, great to slice, and easy to stack.

Preheat the oven to 375°F.

Lightly brush a skillet with the oil, Working in batches, add the eggplant slices and cook for a few minutes on each side until browned and slightly soft.

To make the stacks, arrange 4 slices of eggplant apart in the baking dish. Add 1 slice of tomato to each one, then 1 slice of cheese. Repeat until each stack has 3 slices of eggplant, 2 of tomato, and 3 of cheese, ending with a cheese slice on top. Sprinkle each stack with olive oil.

Bake for about 15 minutes until soft, bubbly, and golden. Serve hot with a crisp green salad or lightly steamed vegetables.

fresh tomato and herb sauce on grilled polenta

1 cup quick-cooking polenta

sea salt and freshly ground black pepper

fresh tomato and herb sauce

1 lb. vine-ripened tomatoes, peeled, seeded, and finely chopped

2 scallions, finely chopped

1 tablespoon finely chopped flat-leaf parsley

1 tablespoon finely chopped fresh thyme

1/4 cup best-quality extra virgin olive oil, plus extra for sprinkling

sea salt and freshly ground black pepper

mixed salad greens, such as frisée, mizuna, radicchio, and arugula, to serve

a rectangular wooden board, baking sheet or round cake pan, 8 inches diameter, oiled

serves 4

A great dish for late summer, and the raw sauce is very versatile. You can add a couple of drops of balsamic vinegar to bring out the flavor of the tomatoes, or use the sauce as a chunky topping for many dishes from fish to pasta. Just remember that the flavor comes from supremely ripe tomatoes and a full-flavored, extra virgin olive oil—first-pressed and cold-pressed, naturally.

Cook the polenta according to the package instructions, adding a little salt and pepper to the mixture. Pour onto a rectangular wooden board and form into a mound. Alternatively, pour into the cake pan. Let set for at least 1 hour, then cut into 4 slices. If the cooled polenta is too large, slice it in half horizontally, then cut into slices.

To make the sauce, put the tomatoes, scallions, herbs, salt, and pepper in a bowl. Add the olive oil and stir gently. Set aside for about 30 minutes to let the flavors mingle.

Heat a stovetop grill pan until very hot. Working in batches, brush the polenta pieces with olive oil and cook for a few minutes on each side until golden and barred with grill marks. Remove from the pan and keep them warm in a low oven.

Put the polenta onto serving plates, spoon the sauce over the top, sprinkle with extra olive oil and serve with a small salad of mixed greens.

pasta, grains, and beans

tomato and pea risotto

about 3¾ cups vegetable stock*

4 tablespoons unsalted butter

1 baby leek, cleaned and finely chopped

2 cups risotto rice, such as vialone nano, carnaroli, or arborio

⅔ cup dry white wine

½ cup freshly grated Parmesan cheese,

¾ cup peas, fresh or frozen and thawed

10 small, vine-ripened tomatoes, peeled and quartered

about 1 cup freshly chopped mixed herbs, such as thyme, sage, rosemary, fennel, or mint

best-quality extra virgin olive oil, to serve

serves 4

I find the quantity of stock needed will vary, depending on which rice is used. Traditionally, the ratio is said to be about 3 cups stock to 1 cup rice, but here I needed much less. Always keep some extra and use as you require.

I remember watching a leading Italian chef, RoDante, demonstrating risotto made with vialone nano rice, a stunning olive oil, and aromatic herbs at the Petrini olive farm in Italy. Sublime. Having watched a master in action, I've come up with a recipe with wonderful flavor, but which also looks rather pretty with tomato and peas. The secret of maximum tomato flavor depends on beautifully ripe tomatoes added toward the end, so their juices just start to seep into the rich, creamy risotto.

Put the stock in a saucepan and bring to a boil. Reduce the heat and keep simmering gently over low heat.

Melt the butter in a wide, heavy saucepan, add the leek, and sauté until softened but not browned. Add the rice and stir briefly until the grains become translucent around the edges. Turn up the heat, add the wine, and simmer until it evaporates.

Reduce the heat to medium-low and add the very hot stock 1 ladle at a time, until each is absorbed. The rice should have a little bite—it should never be mushy or cooked solid. The Italians say it should flow like a wave—all'onde—when you lift and shake the pan.

After about 15 minutes cooking, add the Parmesan, stir well over low heat, and leave for 1 minute. Add the peas and tomatoes with their juices, and let cook for another few minutes. Put the lid on and turn off the heat. Leave the risotto to rest for 2 minutes, then serve on warm plates. Top with the finely chopped herbs and a generous amount of olive oil.

Note Cooking time may vary with quality of rice, your stove and heat level.

tomato and mint couscous
with feta cheese and white beans

10 oz. red and yellow cherry tomatoes or baby plum tomatoes, such as Elfin

1 1/4 cups couscous

1 1/2 cups hot vegetable stock

1 tablespoon extra virgin olive oil, plus extra for broiling

1 tablespoon butter

15 oz. canned white beans, rinsed and drained well, about 3 cups

4 oz. feta cheese, crumbled

2 tablespoons coarsely chopped mint

sea salt and freshly ground black pepper

serves 4

A Moroccan pasta dish with Greek overtones—a delicious mix that sings of the Mediterranean. Although you can simply soak couscous with hot water or stock poured over, then covered, I prefer mine steamed for an extra few minutes for improved texture.

Put the tomatoes in a bowl, add a little olive oil, salt, and pepper, and toss briefly. Cook under a hot broiler for 2-3 minutes until just tender and the skins have split.

Put the couscous in a large bowl and cover with the hot stock. Add the olive oil, stir once, cover with plastic wrap, and let stand for about 5 minutes. Fluff up with a fork, then put in a fine-meshed stainless steel strainer. Set the strainer over a saucepan of boiling water and steam for a further 5 minutes or until you see a little steam rising through the grains.

Return the couscous to the bowl, add the butter, and fluff up again with a fork until the butter has melted through. Add the beans, feta cheese, and half the mint. Add salt and pepper to taste. Carefully mix in the tomatoes, so they remain whole, and sprinkle with the remaining mint. Serve.

Note Instead of broiling the tomatoes, you can roast them in a preheated oven at 450°F for just 5 minutes.

garlic-baked tomatoes, with pasta, olives, and basil

1 lb. vine-ripened but still firm tomatoes, halved

3 garlic cloves, chopped

24 basil leaves, torn, or a bunch of arugula

1/4 cup extra virgin olive oil, plus extra for sprinkling

14 oz. spaghetti

1/3 cup small black olives, such as Niçoise, pitted and finely chopped

sea salt and freshly ground black pepper

freshly shaved Parmesan cheese, to serve

serves 4

For this recipe, it is essential that the tomatoes aren't roasted until falling apart. They should be just tender, so they keep their shape. Instead of spaghetti, you could use other simple shapes such as linguine or fusilli lunghi (long spirals), but nothing that's too fussy. There's a lot happening on the plate, so keep it simple.

Preheat the oven to 450°F.

Put the tomatoes in an ovenproof dish cut side up. Sprinkle with the garlic, one-third of the basil or arugula, the olive oil, salt, and pepper. Roast for about 8 minutes or until the tomatoes are just tender. Transfer to a plate, together with their cooking oil and juices, and keep them warm.

Bring a large saucepan of lightly salted water to a boil. Add the spaghetti and cook until *al dente*—tender but still firm to the bite. Drain, reserving 1 tablespoon of the pasta water. Return the spaghetti to the pan and add the reserved tablespoon of water. Add the chopped olives, the remaining basil or arugula, and the hot oil and juices from the tomatoes. Season with salt and plenty of pepper and toss well, using 2 forks.

Serve the spaghetti in heated pasta bowls with the tomatoes and Parmesan shavings on top.

chickpea and tomato masala
with beans and cilantro

1 thick slice fresh ginger, chopped

2 garlic cloves, coarsely chopped

2 tablespoons safflower oil

1/4 teaspoon ground turmeric

3 fresh green chiles, halved

1 teaspoon cumin seeds

1 onion, halved lengthwise,
then sliced into half-rings

8 oz. green beans, trimmed

2 cans chickpeas, 15 oz. each,
rinsed and drained, about 5 cups

a pinch of ground cloves

a pinch of ground cinnamon

1 teaspoon ground coriander

1/4 teaspoon ground cumin

8 oz. cherry tomatoes, quartered

sea salt and freshly
ground black pepper

to serve

chopped cilantro leaves (optional)

Indian bread, such as
pooris, chapattis, naan bread,
or buttered pita breads

serves 4–6

A satisfying dish with Indian flavors in which, instead of a typically smooth tomato-based sauce, cherry tomatoes are folded in at the last moment. It is based on chole or channa masala, a great Indian vegetarian dish.

Using a mortar and pestle, mash the ginger and garlic to a chunky paste. Heat the oil in a saucepan, add the turmeric, chiles, and cumin seeds, and sauté briefly. Add the onions and sauté for about 6 minutes. Add the ginger and garlic paste and sauté for 2–3 minutes more until the onions have softened.

Add the green beans and 1/2 cup water, then bring to a boil. Lower the heat and cook gently for 10 minutes. Add the chickpeas, ground cloves, cinnamon, coriander, and cumin. Add salt and pepper to taste, and mix well. Cook for 9 minutes more. Gently fold in the cherry tomatoes with a wooden spoon. Turn off the heat, cover, and steam for 1–2 minutes. Sprinkle with chopped cilantro, if using, and serve with Indian breads or buttered pita breads.

Variation In India, chickpeas are usually cooked in a tomato sauce. If you would like to prepare the the dish this way, add canned chopped tomatoes after adding the green beans. You may not need any extra water, because the canned tomatoes have plenty of juice. You can also put the tomatoes in a food processor and blend briefly, leaving some texture, before pouring over the beans.

bloody mary

1 cup vodka

2 cups tomato juice

3 1/2 – 4 tablespoons lemon juice

1/2 teaspoon Tabasco sauce, or to taste

1 teaspoon Worcestershire sauce, or to taste

a pinch of freshly ground white pepper

to serve

ice cubes

4 celery stalks

a few finely chopped celery leaves (optional)

serves 4

Bloody Mary is the perfect drink to serve with brunch or a summer lunch (and who could fault the robust combination of tomatoes, vodka, Tabasco, and Worcestershire sauce as the world's greatest hangover cure?).

Put the vodka, tomato juice, lemon juice, Tabasco sauce, Worcestershire sauce, and pepper in a large pitcher and stir well. Pour into 4 glasses filled with ice cubes. Add a celery stalk to and sprinkle with a few chopped celery leaves, if using. Serve.

Alternatively, use a cocktail mixer partially filled with ice cubes. Shake well, strain into the pitcher, then serve as above.

salsa roja with tomato and jalapeño

1 1/2 lb. vine-ripened tomatoes, peeled, seeded and chopped

1 medium white onion, finely chopped

2 large garlic cloves, finely chopped

2 fresh jalapeño chiles, seeded and finely chopped or 2 tablespoons jalapeño slices in vinegar, rinsed, drained, and chopped

freshly squeezed juice of 1/2 lime

sea salt

serves 6–8

The classic Mexican red salsa. Make it with a ripe, top variety of tomato, bursting with sweetness and flavor, like those found at roadside stands in late August. Fresh jalapeños are widely available, but you can use sliced ones packed in vinegar (saving the vinegar for other recipes), though they won't be as good.

Put all the ingredients in a bowl, mix well, and let marinate for 30 minutes before serving.

tomato additions

slow-cooked tomato and basil sauce

2 tablespoons extra virgin olive oil

3 large garlic cloves, crushed

3 lb. vine-ripened plum tomatoes, such as Roma or San Marzano, peeled, seeded, and chopped

1 teaspoon sugar

20 large basil leaves

sea salt and freshly ground black pepper

serves 4

A good tomato sauce is essential in a tomato book, so here it is—a dark, rich sauce, full of summer goodness and basil fragrance. It is perfect tossed through spaghetti or to accompany meat or vegetable dishes. Ripe, sweet, flavorful tomatoes are the key to its success.

Heat the olive oil in a heavy saucepan, add the garlic, and sauté for 1 minute. Add the chopped tomatoes and sugar and stir well. Tear half the basil into pieces, then add to the saucepan. Add salt and pepper to taste, bring to a boil, and simmer gently for about 45 minutes or until the tomatoes are soft and the sauce has thickened. Tear the remaining basil and add to the sauce just before serving. Use immediately, or keep in the refrigerator for up to 2 days, or freeze.

Note The longer the tomatoes cook over low heat, the more concentrated the flavor.

tomato and ginger chutney

2 tablespoons safflower oil

6 scallions, chopped

1 inch fresh ginger, sliced into thin, small strips, about ½-inch long

1¾ lb. tomatoes, peeled

⅓ cup raisins

⅓ cup white wine vinegar

¼ cup sugar

a preserving pan or large stainless steel saucepan

1 glass jar with lid, sterilized, about 2 cups (page 4)

serves 6–8 in small portions

This is a favorite sweet Indian chutney, enjoyed throughout the Subcontinent and in chutney-mad Britain. It is tangy and sweet, but sharp with ginger at the same time. Green tomato chutneys or hot pickles are also enjoyed in India, Pakistan, and Bangladesh—there, it is the sourness of the green fruit that is most relished. Experiment with both kinds as they are equally good. Serve with Indian dishes, cold or potted meats, sandwiches, cheese, or salads.

Put the oil, scallions, ginger, tomatoes, raisins, and vinegar in a preserving pan or non-reactive saucepan and bring to a boil. Reduce the heat and simmer gently for 45 minutes–1 hour.

Add the sugar and continue to cook until thickened. Transfer to the sterilized jar, seal tightly, and store until completely cold and set. Keep in a cool, dark place.

Note The chutney will thicken further when cool.

oven-dried tomatoes

1 lb. vine-ripened small-fruited tomatoes, such as Elfin or Juliette

1/2 garlic clove, sliced into thin slivers

extra virgin olive oil

sea salt and cracked black pepper

serves 4

To dry tomatoes fully in the oven, you'd have to bake them forever, or at least a day or two. It is an alternative to drying naturally under the hot sun—but why bother when sun-dried tomatoes are readily available? Instead, try this easy idea, crinkly but juicy and deliciously garlicky. Cook at high temperature at the start to caramelize the edges, then dry them out in a low even. So easy. If you are serving them as party food—just double or quadruple the recipe as needed.

Preheat the oven to 475°F or its highest temperature.

Cut the tomatoes in half lengthwise and remove the cores but not the juice. Put them cut side up onto a baking sheet, season lightly with salt and pepper, top each half with a few garlic slivers, and sprinkle with the olive oil.

Bake for about 10 minutes or until they just start to collapse. Lower the heat to 275°F and cook for 50 minutes more. Remove and let cool.

Serve as a side dish, finger food, or as a appetizer.

sun-dried tomato oil

Simple sun-dried tomato oil has many uses. It will enhance the flavor of these colorful grilled vegetables, and the vegetables can be chosen to suit your mood. You can also use the oil on a salad, over pasta or even with chunky soft bread, such as focaccia. It's a handy condiment.

³/₄ cup extra virgin olive oil

1-2 small fresh red chiles, quartered

1 garlic clove, sliced

6 sun-dried tomatoes, rehydrated according to package instructions, drained and finely chopped

a small bunch of chives, chopped

sea salt and freshly ground black pepper

grilled vegetables

a handful of mushrooms, halved

12 asparagus tips, lightly blanched

1 zucchini, halved, then sliced lengthwise into wide strips

1 large white onion, cut into wedges

1 red bell pepper, seeded and cut into wide strips

1 yellow or orange bell pepper, seeded and cut into wide strips

2 green bell peppers, seeded and cut into wide strips

a handful of cherry tomatoes, pricked

serves 4

To make the dressing, pour the olive oil into a saucepan and add the chile quarters and garlic slices. Gently warm over low heat for a few minutes. Do not boil or simmer. Remove the chile quarters. Add the sun-dried tomatoes and chives, and lightly season with salt and pepper. Stir well, then set aside until ready to use.

To prepare the vegetables, put the mushrooms, asparagus, zucchini, onion, bell peppers, and cherry tomatoes in a bowl. Add a few tablespoons of the sun-dried tomato oil and toss well until the vegetables are coated. Working in batches if necessary, arrange the vegetables in a single layer on a broiler pan and broil until lightly charred in places, tender, and warmed through. When broiling the vegetables, keep watching them as some may cook quicker than others.

Transfer the vegetables to a warmed bowl and sprinkle generously with more of the sun-dried tomato oil. Mix well to make sure that all the vegetables are coated. Taste and adjust the seasoning if necessary.

Serve the remaining oil separately with bread.

Notes

• Use this homemade flavored oil soon after making. Otherwise store in the refrigerator and use within 1-2 days.

• The soaking water from the tomatoes can be used to flavor foods too.

peanut and tomato raita

3 cups plain yogurt

2-3 fresh green chiles, such as jalapeño or serrano seeded and finely chopped

1 lb. vine-ripened but still firm tomatoes, peeled and chopped

about 2 cups chopped cilantro, plus extra to serve

1/2 cup pan-toasted peanuts (unsalted), coarsely crushed, plus extra to serve

2 tablespoons peanut oil

a pinch of ground chile powder

a pinch of ground turmeric

1 teaspoon black mustard seeds

1/2 teaspoon cumin seeds

a few fresh curry leaves (optional)

sea salt

serves 8

This has to be my all-time favorite raita (savory spiced yogurt). It's always a hit. It comes from Maharashtra in western India, where people just love peanuts. In India, housewives don't bother to peel the tomatoes for this raita, but I usually do. Keep the juice and seeds, so all their flavor seeps into the raita. Serve the raita with spicy entrées and side dishes.

Put the yogurt in a bowl and if it is slightly lumpy, beat with a fork until smooth. Add the chiles, tomatoes, cilantro, and peanuts and mix well.

Heat the oil in a small skillet. Add the chile, turmeric, mustard seeds, cumin seeds, and curry leaves, if using, and cover. Let cook briefly until the seeds crackle and pop. Remove from the heat, uncover, and immediately pour over the raita, scraping the pan to remove all the spices and oil. Beat well with a small whisk. Serve topped with extra chopped peanuts and cilantro.

tomato and cucumber kosumbri

1 tablespoon cumin seeds

3 vine-ripened but still firm plum tomatoes, finely chopped

1 small cucumber, seeded and finely chopped

1/2 teaspoon dried crushed red chiles

1/4 teaspoon brown sugar or a pinch of jaggery (palm sugar)

2 tablespoons chopped cilantro

3 tablespoons lemon juice

a few mint leaves, freshly torn or chopped

sea salt

serves 6

Kosumbri is a typical South Indian salad, but here it is served in bite-size portions, as a condiment. There are a number of variations on the theme and this is a typical, refreshing kosumbri, ideal for the hot summer months.

Put the cumin seeds in a dry skillet and cook until lightly toasted and fragrant. Remove to a plate and let cool.

Put the tomatoes, cucumber, toasted cumin seeds, chiles, sugar, cilantro, lemon juice, mint, and salt in a bowl and mix well. Serve in small portions with entrées.

Note Although I seed the cucumber, I like the flavor of the tomato seeds and juices in this salad—and usually these are left in when served at home. The bright colors of the tomato and cucumber skins also make for a pretty salad, but again, if you require sophistication, peel both.

index

conversion chart

Weights and measures have been rounded up or down slightly to make measuring easier.

volume equivalents:

american	metric	imperial
1 teaspoon		5 ml
1 tablespoon	15 ml	
¼ cup	60 ml	2 fl.oz.
⅓ cup	75 ml	2½ fl.oz.
½ cup	125 ml	4 fl.oz.
⅔ cup	150 ml	5 fl.oz. (¼ pint)
¾ cup	175 ml	6 fl.oz.
1 cup	250 ml	8 fl.oz.

weight equivalents:

imperial	metric
1 oz.	25 g
2 oz.	50 g
3 oz.	75 g
4 oz.	125 g
5 oz.	150 g
6 oz.	175 g
7 oz.	200 g
8 oz.	250 g
9 oz.	275 g
10 oz.	300 g
11 oz.	325 g
12 oz.	375 g
13 oz.	400 g
14 oz.	425 g
15 oz.	475 g
16 oz. (1 lb.)	500 g
2 lb.	1 kg

measurements:

inches	cm
¼ inch	5 mm
½ inch	1 cm
¾ inch	1.5 cm
1 inch	2.5 cm
2 inches	5 cm
3 inches	7 cm
4 inches	10 cm
5 inches	12 cm
6 inches	15 cm
7 inches	18 cm
8 inches	20 cm
9 inches	23 cm
10 inches	25 cm
11 inches	28 cm
12 inches	30 cm

oven temperatures:

225°F	110°C	Gas ¼
250°F	120°C	Gas ½
275°F	140°C	Gas 1
300°F	150°C	Gas 2
325°F	160°C	Gas 3
350°F	180°C	Gas 4
375°F	190°C	Gas 5
400°F	200°C	Gas 6
425°F.	220°C	Gas 7
450°F	230°C	Gas 8
475°F	240°C	Gas 9